# Doing and Rewarding

# The Master Management Series

## William F. Christopher
### Editor-in-Chief

6

# Doing and Rewarding

## Inside a High-Performance Organization

Carl G. Thor

PRODUCTIVITY PRESS

Portland, Oregon

Volume 6 of the *Management Master Series*.
William F. Christopher, Editor-in-Chief
Copyright © 1994 by Productivity Press, Inc.

Productivity Press
P.O. Box 13390
Portland OR 97213-0390
United States of America
Telephone: 503-235-0600
Telefax: 503-235-0909

ISBN: 1-56327-061-7

Book design by William Stanton
Composition by Rohani Design
Printed and bound by BookCrafters in the United States of America

*Library of Congress Cataloging-in-Publication Data*

Thor, Carl G.
    Doing and rewarding : inside a high-performance organization / Carl G. Thor.
       p.   cm. -- (Management master series ; v. 6)
    Includes bibliographical references.
    ISBN 1-56327-061-7
    1. Work groups.  2. Performance.  3. Achievement motivation.
4. Industrial organization.  I. Title.  II. Series.
HD66.T49   1994
658.4'036--dc20
                                    94-22589
                                       CIP

98 97 96 95     10 9 8 7 6 5 4 3 2

# —CONTENTS—

Publisher's Message  vii

1. Prerequisites for High Performance  1

   High Performance and Team Effectiveness  1

2. Operating in an Employee Involvement Culture  4

   A Closer Look at Involvement and Performance  4
   Components of Employee Involvement  7

3. How Teams Operate Effectively  12

   Special Purpose Teams  12
   Permanent Operating Teams  16
   Measuring Teams  18
   Recognizing Teams  21

4. Gainsharing: The Path to High Performance  24

   What Is Gainsharing?  24
   Creating a Customized Plan  28
   Limitations of Gainsharing  43

5. Summary and Conclusion  45

Bibliography  47
About the Author  48

# PUBLISHER'S MESSAGE

The *Management Master Series* was designed to discover and disseminate to you the world's best concepts, principles, and current practices in excellent management. We present this information in a concise and easy-to-use format to provide you with the tools and techniques you need to stay abreast of this rapidly accelerating world of ideas.

World class competitiveness requires managers today to be thoroughly informed about how and what other internationally successful managers are doing. What works? What doesn't? and Why?

Management is often considered a "neglected art." It is not possible to know how to manage before you are made a manager. But once you become a manager you are expected to know how to manage and to do it well, right from the start.

One result of this neglect in management training has been managers who rely on control rather than creativity. Certainly, managers in this century have shown a distinct neglect of workers as creative human beings. The idea that employees are an organization's most valuable asset is still very new. How managers can inspire and direct the creativity and intelligence of everyone involved in the work of an organization has only begun to emerge.

Perhaps if we consider management as a "science" the task of learning how to manage well will be easier. A scientist begins with an hypothesis and then runs experiments to observe whether the hypothesis is correct. Scientists depend on detailed notes about the experiment—the timing, the ingredients, the amounts—and carefully record all results as they test new hypotheses. Certain things come to be known by this method; for instance, that water always consists of one part oxygen and two parts hydrogen.

We as managers must learn from our experience and from the experience of others. The scientific approach provides a model for learning. Science begins with vision and desired outcomes, and achieves its purpose through observation, experiment, and analysis of precisely recorded results. And then what is newly discovered is shared so that each person's research will build on the work of others.

Our organizations, however, rarely provide the time for learning or experimentation. As a manager, you need information from those who have already experimented and learned and recorded their results. You need it in brief, clear, and detailed form so that you can apply it immediately.

It is our purpose to help you confront the difficult task of managing in these turbulent times. As the shape of leadership changes, the *Management Master Series* will continue to bring you the best learning available to support your own increasing artistry in the evolving science of management.

We at Productivity Press are grateful to William F. Christopher and our staff of editors who have searched out those masters with the knowledge, experience, and ability to write concisely and completely on excellence in management practice. We wish also to thank the individual volume authors; Cheryl Rosen and Diane Asay, project managers; Julie Zinkus, manuscript editor; Karen Jones, managing editor; Lisa Hoberg, Mary Junewick, and Julie Hankin, editorial support; Bill Stanton, design and production management; Susan Swanson, production coordination; Rohani Design, composition.

Norman Bodek
Publisher

# 1

## PREREQUISITES FOR HIGH PERFORMANCE

An organization does not suddenly become *high-performance* overnight. The organization and its key executives have prepared for years, putting in place a large number of systems, habits, and special characteristics. This organizational culture and management style are at least partly different in each high-performer, but some vital, common threads can be isolated and analyzed.

### HIGH PERFORMANCE AND TEAM EFFECTIVENESS

The emphasis of this discussion is to look at how a high-performer operates routinely on a day-to-day basis. Understanding this type of effective operation, however, requires clarification of the underlying models and assumptions that are prerequisite to smooth operation.

The model in Figure 1 puts several key ideas together in a mutual relationship with *team effectiveness*. This is the perceived local aspect of a high-performance organization that draws comment and admiration.[8] As we will see below, in addition, some evidence shows that effective local team activity is closely related to big-picture measures of organizational success.

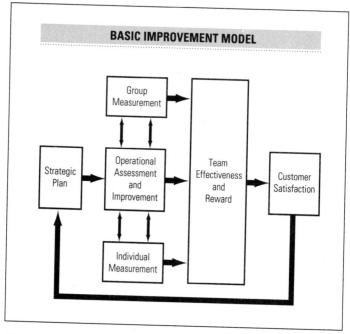

**Figure 1.**

## Customer Satisfaction

A critical part of the model, which is for many people the starting point, is satisfying the customer. Without customers there is no business to justify the organization's existence. Dissatisfied customers will not keep buying once there is an alternative. However, this is oversimplified. Most businesses have many potential customers of different types with conflicting needs and expectations. Therefore, only some aspects of customer satisfaction can be handled by *systems* of uniform offering and treatment. One of the common features of a high-performance organization is the ability of flexible and alert employees to separately satisfy each customer's varying need without incurring prohibitive cost.

## Strategic Planning

Another critical part of the model, and an alternative starting point, is active strategic planning that blends the capabilities and desires of the organization's leadership and ownership with the major customer needs. It is appropriate to think of the planning system as a funnel that delivers a select few of the many varying customer ideas to the operational organization for focused assessment and improvement action.

Accompanying the action priorities must be a measurement system that lets those charged with improvement see if it is in fact happening and to guide them in making mid-course corrections if it is not. The measurement system includes information on the performance of groups (departments and cross-cutting processes) and individuals (executives and nonexecutive employees) that can help the responsible teams manage their activities.

## Leadership Style

Implicit in Figure 1 are two important pieces of leadership style: competitive drive and coaching mentality. Leaders must recognize the dynamics of the world around them and routinely be prepared to act vigorously to reach out to customers and to adjust strategies to meet emerging competitive threats. Leaders must also be able to delegate responsibility to the lower levels of the organization and let them go ahead without micromanagement. An employee involvement culture cannot be occasional and conditional. It must be the way everyone in the organization operates.

An organization whose situation is similar to that outlined above is likely to be a high-performance organization. Their teams will be effective, their customers will be satisfied, their plans will be met, and rewards will be there for everyone. The remainder of this discussion demonstrates how such an organization operates and, especially, how it can reward its successful doers.

# 2

## OPERATING IN AN EMPLOYEE INVOLVEMENT CULTURE

The link between employee involvement and organizational performance is taken on faith by believers and nonbelievers alike. Nonbelievers feel that an organization succeeds only because of the technical skill and wisdom of a few key people, who must carefully watch the rest of the workforce and lead them step-by-step to an acceptable level of performance. This attracts mainly dullards to an organization and its pre-orientation is easy to demonstrate. Believers, however, know that real employee involvement makes a big difference. When the word gets around an organization truly empowers its employees to go beyond their starting capabilities, bright and ambitious people want to join that organization.

### A CLOSER LOOK AT INVOLVEMENT AND PERFORMANCE

A study conducted by the Center for Effective Organizations of the University of Southern California, and published by the American Productivity and Quality Center in 1989 has brought some rigor to the faith-driven statement above.[1] In responses from 476 large companies to the original survey, 82 percent indicated some form of employee involvement practices. Those with such practices were asked to indicate the impact of employee involvement on various performance indicators. Figure 2 shows that 68 to 76 percent indicated a

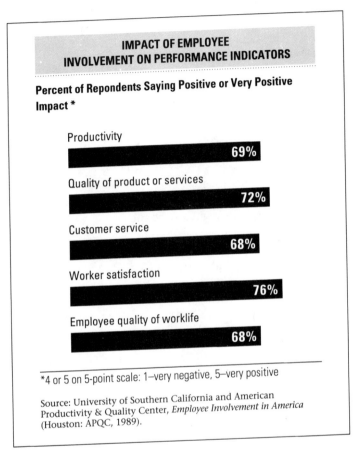

**IMPACT OF EMPLOYEE INVOLVEMENT ON PERFORMANCE INDICATORS**

Percent of Repondents Saying Positive or Very Positive Impact *

Productivity
**69%**

Quality of product or services
**72%**

Customer service
**68%**

Worker satisfaction
**76%**

Employee quality of worklife
**68%**

*4 or 5 on 5-point scale: 1–very negative, 5–very positive

Source: University of Southern California and American Productivity & Quality Center, *Employee Involvement in America* (Houston: APQC, 1989).

**Figure 2.**

positive or very positive relationship of employee involvement practices to productivity, quality of product or service, customer service and worker satisfaction.

The study's results were further subdivided into high-performer and low-performer groups, based on a self-rating of the impact of employee involvement on performance indicators. The characteristics of the efforts of the high-performance companies were then compared with those that were low performance. The high-performance companies have important distinctions:

- They have been doing it longer.

- Their CEO is more likely to have been the original source.

- They are more likely to have the union(s) involved.

- They have senior management support.

For a newcomer to employee involvement, these characteristics are usually not immediately available. Figure 3 shows tactical differences that might also be critical and more immediately workable.

Note that a major difference between the two groups is that high-performers have written objectives and formal measures of performance, whereas low-performers are unclear in these areas.

---

### TACTICAL DIFFERENCES IN ORGANIZATIONAL PERFORMANCE

High-performance organizations are more likely to have:
- an employee involvement policy
- manual of procedures
- written management objectives
- formal measures
- an internal consulting staff
- external consultants

Low-performance organizations are more likely to:
- have unclear objectives
- lack tangible improvements
- lack a champion

Source: USC/APQC, *Employee Involvement in America* (Houston: APQC, 1989.

**Figure 3.**

# COMPONENTS OF EMPLOYEE INVOLVEMENT

The USC/APQC study and the useful guide to participative methods in the public sector, "Employee Involvement and Quality Management"[4] both classify employee involvement techniques into four categories:

- Information-sharing
- Knowledge/skill/ability
- Rewards/recognition
- Power/authority/accountability

## Information-sharing

Information-sharing typically comes first when an organization begins to practice participative management.

Some common forms of information-sharing are listed below.[4]

- Posting/meetings on operating results, budgets, and competition
- Shared databases and broadened access in information system
- Survey feedback
- Suggestion systems, committees, and results
- Familiarization with new technology
- Internal pay levels, categories, and supplements
- Cross-functional orientation groups and business process identification
- Quality, quality-of-work-life committees and groups
- Job enrichment projects and customer-supplier identification
- Performance feedback sessions
- Information on the work of other teams

Some people sharply criticize limited forms of information-sharing that become the only initiative management can live with. We have all seen bulletin-board displays, originally well-meaning, that have evolved to an almost symbolic statement of the shallowness of a management's commitment. Recognizing that information won't hurt anyone, and that it may make differences in quite unforeseen ways, generates vital momentum that leads to more advanced information-sharing techniques.

## Knowledge/Skill/Ability

Training programs of various types and opportunities to use the new information build knowledge, skills and abilities. Without these opportunities, training programs are nearly useless. Some organizations have training programs that are better classed as indoctrination: "From this moment on, you are all ordered to be participative; just don't overdo it." Others may present useful skills training in an unintentionally demeaning way that discourages (or forbids) experimentation with better methods or ideas. Still others believe that outside scorekeepers are the key to efficient training.

Quality award representatives want to know what percentage of time or cost is spent in training, without regard to appropriateness of the training subject and/or its timing. Most effective organizations use *just-in-time* training, which provides new information only when employees are ready to use it. This has better results than training the whole organization at the same time to demonstrate some ideal in communications and equity. Premature training generates both cynicism and normal human forgetfulness.

Some of the education and skill requirements for a participative organization are presented in Figure 4.

## Rewards/Recognition

For good and bad reasons, organizations often sidestep rewards and recognition. Zealots for employee involvement believe (correctly) that recognition is best when it is an insepa-

---

### KNOWLEDGE/SKILL/ABILITY REQUIREMENTS

- Communication, listening skills and meeting management
- Leadership skills and coaching
- Group decision making and problem solving
- Measurement, statistical analysis and surveys
- Team-building
- Training needs analysis and talent banks
- Cross-training and multi-skilling
- Benchmarking
- Conflict management and negotiation
- Skills in understanding the business and industry

---

**Figure 4.**

rable habit of management and not an awkward and delayed special nuisance. But even the best of people are awkward in learning a new skill, and many managers need help remembering to recognize their employees' developments and triumphs.

Some experts also feel that crass financial rewards for better performance demean the joy of participation and self-discovery. People very often are pleased to try new things and feel good about improvement they have aided. Employee involvement is often accompanied by a decentralization of authority and increased responsibility for ordinary workers. Sometimes the reward for increased responsibility is a higher salary. Recently, however, it has become more common to reward involved employees by letting them keep their jobs, while other, less-flexible (or less senior) employees are downsized out. As employee involvement efforts mature, the *what's in it for me* talk starts again. Using a simple analogy, most people will eat cake with pleasure when it is offered but will smile more broadly or walk further to join in if it is clear the cake is frosted!

Sometimes the very processes used to determine recipients can ruin well-meaning recognitions. Senior executives are allowed to choose their favorites and may veto candidates that workers favor. Also, the delays and checks and balances can be so heavy that busy managers or workers don't have the time to make the required case for recognition. Or, the award is so far off in the future that everyone forgets what it was for.

Organizations may use frugality as a reason to sidestep rewards and recognition. But much recognition costs absolutely nothing, and even many of the tangible rewards pay for themselves. A later section of this volume presents a thorough discussion of gainsharing. This is one of the major forms of tangible reward on a group or team basis. Other approaches to rewards and recognition are listed in Figure 5.

## Power/Authority/Accountability

The most subtle component of employee involvement, both hardest to measure and most important, is employee empowerment. Senior management must pass on true power and authority to employees who must accept the new responsibility and accountability. In the USC/APQC study, only 28

---

### APPROACHES TO REWARDS AND RECOGNITION

- Individual incentives
- Merit pay
- Profit sharing
- Gainsharing
- Stock ownership
- All-salaried pay
- Knowledge/skill-based pay
- Flexible benefits
- Suggestion systems
- Lump-sum performance bonus
- Employee and/or team-of-the-month rewards or recognition
- Sabbatical leave, special project, and education leave/subsidy
- Extraordinary equipment, office, and other perquisites
- Caps, jackets and other paraphernalia

---

**Figure 5.**

percent of the respondents had any experience with self-managed work teams, the most interesting of the power-sharing approaches. Three-quarters of them had less than 20 percent of their employees working in that form. Only 11 percent of the respondents indicated that a great or very great shift had occurred to the extent that decision making had moved to a lower level in the organization.

The common denominator of all these techniques can be summed up in two phrases: organizational flexibility and respect for each worker's potential. Organizations in this mode are able to offer and practice employment security (but not necessarily job security) and join the ranks of world-class competitors.

# 3

## HOW TEAMS
## OPERATE EFFECTIVELY

Though the organization's involvement culture has much to do with the success of a team-based organization, the structure in which the teams operate is important also. There are different challenges and cautions for different types of teams. There is a major difference between special purpose teams and permanent operating teams.

### SPECIAL PURPOSE TEAMS

The first experience for most people with teams is with a special purpose team set up temporarily outside of the normal administrative structure of the organization. Special purpose teams may be established to address a community issue, or, for example, the creation of a gainsharing plan. At least five distinct types of special purpose teams can be described (see Figure 6).

---

**TYPES OF SPECIAL PURPOSE TEAMS**

- Quality Circles
- Problem-Solving Teams/Task Forces
- Customer/Supplier Teams
- Benchmarking Teams
- Labor/Management Teams

---

**Figure 6.**

## Quality Circles

In the late '70s and early '80s many organizations, reflecting stories from Japan, established Quality Circles. There are many variations, but they are typically small groups of six to ten co-workers who meet voluntarily during company time to analyze local problems and recommend improvements. The individuals usually have a small amount of training in group processes and some of the key problem-solving techniques (Pareto analysis, cause-and-effect diagrams, graphing, etc.). Initially, supervisors or trained leaders from the corporate staff facilitate these circles. Often, however, some of the more active circle members take additional training and become facilitators themselves.

Quality Circles may meet for an hour or two every one or two weeks. They usually select their own problems to address. Often they start off with small annoyances or cosmetic projects, but move on to fairly important process improvements or micro-reorganizations of work. Their scope usually ends at the boundaries of their work group.

Most of an organization's truly major problems are cross-departmental, and Quality Circles rarely have a charter or a makeup that allows such wide-ranging work. Their voluntary nature also limits their scope. Initially half or more of the local employees may belong to a circle, but when the circles mature for a year or two, and the easy issues have been addressed, membership falls back to 20 percent or less of those eligible. In retrospect, many organizations now say that the main value of Quality Circles was as a warm-up exercise for some of the more advanced forms of employee involvement. The hard-core 20 percent from Quality Circles have gone on to become the leaders of the next phases of improvement. Even the 80 percent who dropped out or never joined got an inkling of what the new world of employee involvement would be like, for better or for worse.

## Problem-Solving Teams

A second form of special purpose team, which builds on some of the problems of Quality Circles, is the Problem-Solving

Team or Task Force. This type of team attacks a major, cross-cutting problem in the organization. Membership is from all concerned parts of the organization, is non-voluntary, and usually involves high to medium level managers or technical specialists. When you see the word *Task Force* expect managers; when you see the word *Team* in this context, expect at least some nonmanagement people to be involved.

A Problem-Solving Team is a parallel organization. It is a temporary and, usually, part-time assignment whose members retain much or all of their normal responsibilities, at least on paper. In practice, the members' subordinates end up with extra work while the managers become special Problem Solvers. Median duration of these teams or task forces may be three to five months, with a range of one month to one year. Typically members spend 25 to 50 percent of their time on the project. In some cases some of the team members may end up with new job assignments at the end of the project, often related to the project recommendations.

## Customer and Supplier Teams

A third type of team, the Customer or Supplier Team, often starts as a Problem-Solving Team focused on one customer or supplier. As the Problem-Solving Team solves, or at least institutionalizes, the special problem that prompted the team's creation, the team, or a lower-level version of it, is kept in being to communicate periodically with the supplier or customer involved in the original problem to prevent any further problems from becoming big enough to need special solutions. The most progressive version of this idea merges the customer team with the sales-marketing team that manages that account on a day-to-day basis. In this case, the team is no longer special purpose, but becomes a permanent operating team.

## Benchmarking Teams

A fourth type of special purpose team of recent creation is the Benchmarking Team. Here the focus is usually on a cross-cutting business process rather than a specific customer or supplier problem. As with a Task Force, a company creates a Benchmarking Team for a single project and then dissolves it. Through planning and prioritization exercises, a company identifies a process that needs attention, then creates a Benchmarking Team to conduct a wide-range benchmarking study on it. Either the process is very important to the organization, or data (or executive intuition) suggests that the organization's performance in this area is not as good as it should be, compared to similar processes in other organizations. Most *support* processes are sufficiently generic to allow most organizations to learn something from each other, even if they are in quite different industries.

The Benchmarking Team should be composed of a few people who actively participate in the current process but from different perspectives. Their role is to bring realism into the study. They clearly understand what is being done currently especially if it is different from the procedures manual (as it usually is). They also have good judgment of what might be possible in the future under changed (more customer-driven) assumptions. These operating people are supplemented by technical and professional specialists who bring the necessary understanding of process technology, human resources issues and legal constraints, measures and accounting data, and information resources outside the company. Together they must define the current process in words, flowcharts, and measures of performance. They also gather customer input on what deliverables are desired under what conditions. They search the outside world for information on how others have done the same process. They then contact other organizations they feel might offer something to learn and arrange to trade information in a systematic and mutually beneficial manner. Last, and far from least, they propose modifications to the existing process based on what they learned, then lead the installation of the changes. During implementation it is very helpful to have staff from the floor on the team to deflect resistance to change.

### Labor/Management Team

The last kind of special purpose team is the Labor/Management Team. Labor and management often work together on the other four types of teams and on the permanent operating teams, but a Labor/Management Team gets a specific job done that is tangible and well-defined. Companies create a Labor/Management Team primarily (and transparently) as a forum for improving labor/management relations short of the bargaining table. Obviously, most of these teams are in unionized companies, but highly structured non-unionized companies occasionally may also find this type of team useful. The teams should be a well-balanced mix between labor and management and include rank-and-file individuals from both sides — not just top union officials and top managers. Rank-and-file members can help keep meetings focused on real issues and prevent meetings that look too much like the bargaining table. These teams might be organized on a semi-permanent basis, meeting every two weeks or every month indefinitely, except for some rotation of membership, with the agenda being fairly general.

## PERMANENT OPERATING TEAMS

Some teams are designed to stay in existence as a part of routine operations (see Figure 7).

---

#### TYPES OF PERMANENT OPERATING TEAMS

- Renamed section or department (not really a team)
- Lightly managed teams
- Work cell (Group Technology)
- Self-managed teams

**Figure 7.**

## Renamed Section or Department

The most common team is still the renamed section or department that has not yet learned to act as a team. Typically, in the early days of conversion to participative management, the order goes out that coworkers will now become teammates or associates; the old staff meeting will now be called team meeting. A team is not a team, though, until there is at least occasional cooperation. Coworkers must help accomplish each others' tasks and pass to members some of the leadership functions previously reserved for the formal leader(s).

## Lightly Managed Teams

A lightly managed team is usually created during the transition from hierarchy to self-management, which usually takes many years. It is a team in which the members, to a great degree, act more on their own initiative and cooperatively. But the team still has a formal reporting relationship to a boss and gets more than just planning direction from above.

Outside the bounds of this team would be:

- major goal setting (team is more milestone oriented)

- hiring and firing

- performance reviews

- new investment and budget issues

- training policies and plans (team would recommend and schedule)

- main schedule parameters (team would do detailed schedule)

- process modification approval (team generates ideas)

- major recognition issues

## Work Cells

A third type of permanent team is the work cell. Under the concept of group technology, a major part of a previously linear production process is located together in such a way that essentially eliminates materials handling and scheduling delays. The machines in the cell are dedicated to the work of that cell only, which perhaps sacrifices some potential economies-of-scale on that machine's work but eliminates costly handling and waiting time. Many cells become self-managed teams, but cells can be in the lightly managed mode also. They are characterized by their form of highly cooperative work rather than their organizational structure.

## Self-Managed Teams

The fourth form of permanent team is the self-managed team. As the name implies, they manage themselves. In the ultimate realization, the only inputs to the team are a place to work, tools and equipment, a set of broad policy and budget guidelines, and a macro-schedule. Outputs from a self-managed team are the required units of product or service. In this context, the team takes responsibility for:

- hiring and training

- work rules and discipline

- scheduling of people and product

- performance review and adjustment

- solving supplier/customer problems (up to the point where they decide they need executive help)

- improvement recommendations on product design and process investment.

Many self-managed teams work with their internal suppliers and customers on the basis of *contracts*: they deliver the product or service at a certain cost, time and specification. In many respects they operate as if they were a legal subsidiary of the parent company. They just happen to be located in the middle of the parent company's plant or office. They may even have a bonus plan based on results as if they were a separate entity.

---

**TYPES OF TEAM MEASURES**

- Customer perception of a team and its work (moment of truth)
- Internal calculations on actual work (upstream excellence)
- Team characteristics and operation (team itself)

---

**Figure 8.**

## MEASURING TEAMS

Three general types of measures can be used to measure a team of any kind. The relative importance of each category varies with the type of team and the company culture, but all three are always present (see Figure 8).

### Customer Perception of the Team and Its Work (Moment of Truth)

Customers perceive the team and its work at the *moment of truth* when it delivers the product or service. If the main customers are outside the organization, this is a little tricky. Surveys provide occasional, general input, but they are subject to response bias and can be doctored in various ways. Third-party interviewers can be used but this is expensive and can annoy the customer. Facts are available around customer rejects, returns, misdeliveries and the like, but it is not always clear where in the chain-of-events the fault lies, and measuring nothing but negatives is discouraging.

### Internal Calculations on Actual Work (Upstream Excellence)

Customer-based data must be supplemented with internally developed data on what actually happened before delivery (*upstream* from the moment of truth). The customer's perception counts heavily, but it can be factually wrong. The problem may be correctable without internal changes in process or procedure. Whether or not the customer is watching a particular result, a company must take internal measures of such things as:

- process cost and labor productivity

- scrap/yield and rework

- on-time, intermediate and total cycle times

- process equipment utilization

- safety

- energy use

- inventory level

- mis-routings

The team uses the data thus derived to correct their own processes and procedures (if it is within their power to do so).

## Team Characteristics and Operation

Finally, there are useful measures of team characteristics and operation. Outsiders tend to emphasize the more tangible measures of team outcomes and results from both the customer's and the internal executive observers' point of view. The team may benefit the most, however, from measures of whether it operates according to its own methods and plans. These measures include:

- the degree of multi-job capability that members of the team hold and use

- the level at which certain types of decisions are made

- absenteeism and turnover

- team meeting attendance

- suggestions/modifications the team makes

- sub-process cycle times

- training intensity and new skill retention

- utilization of tools and equipment

- desire and willingness to go to work

Those new to employee involvement usually emphasize internal executive measures. As their orientation toward quality evolves, customer measures take on equal (and eventually, greater) importance. As the teams approach self-management, the dominant measures become the team-operation measures. The other measures have become second-nature and are automatically considered and adjustments taken. Self-criticism merits some serious thought during time the team sets aside for it.

## RECOGNIZING TEAMS

Forms of recognition tend to evolve in parallel with degrees of involvement. The only recognition that every organization has is some form of individual appraisal. Each employee is periodically reviewed at least to determine whether they should be kept on the payroll. Increasingly, the reviews are formal and structured with a scorecard that the supervisor discusses with the worker. Many of the characteristics on the scorecard have little to do with what the worker needs to do on the job. But they provide a false sense of comfortable objectivity (and legal protection) to unprepared managers.

As organizations mature they make such reviews more frequent and less formal, with an emphasis on two-way criticism. It is not just what the worker can do better but also what the boss can do to help the employee work better. The review of historical events becomes, equally, a look into the future, with emphasis on additional training that might be helpful, or other jobs that the worker might prepare for.

### Merit Increases

Yet to be developed in most organizations is the decoupling of job performance and *merit* wage increases. Historically, most merit increases have had little to do with merit. Everyone gets a 3.5 percent increase (allegedly based on merit), even though it just happens that this year's inflation is running about 3.5 percent.

Most meritorious activity should be recognized with a one-time bonus, rather than a permanent wage increase. If some are *permanently* underpaid, promote them or give them a voluntary raise without distorting either the merit or the inflation-adjustment system. If merit is something special, presumably only a few (15 to 20 percent) should get special recognition.

## Profit Sharing

Companies often use profit sharing as a way to recognize, not only the individual worker, but also the whole organization. Many companies have profit-sharing plans that no one criticizes because they are free money, but the same money could have been used much more effectively. Because the senior executives may have all the money they need for current spending, they assume everyone would like profit-sharing proceeds deferred until retirement. Did anyone ask the workers? Companies use profit as the basis of determining whether a reward is deserved, but they often retain the option to adjust or correct distortions in the accounting system. This can degenerate into an executive-discretion payment, for which no one, executive or worker, has any respect. But, after all, it is free money. Most workers know whether an organization is really doing well because they are in a better position to

| MEASURING AND REWARDING PERFORMANCE | | |
|---|---|---|
| **Where** | **Based On** | **How** |
| Individual | Formal appraisal | Raise, bonus, training |
| Teams, groups departments, plants | (Custom-designed measures??) | (Gainsharing ??) |
| Whole company | Profit | Deferred cash or stock |

**Figure 9.**

understand and observe the physical indicators of performance down on the floor. It would be better for everyone if companies based group rewards on indicators that everyone accepts as real. Also, the payout should be current, when most of the recipients want the money.

## Team of the Month Awards

Many companies have attempted to institute group or team rewards (see Figure 9). Some are very effective. Companies have made good (and bad) use of team competitions that recognize team-of-the-month's accomplishments (and all other teams are *losers*). Teams receive caps and jackets, dinners, ballgame tickets, and load-your-shopping-cart orgies. But most serious team scholars weakly claim that the thrill of participation is its own reward.

# 4

## GAINSHARING: THE PATH TO HIGH PERFORMANCE

Not enough serious attention has been given to gainsharing as a reward system at the team and plant or office level. It treats participants as adults, does not warp their enthusiasm and creates additional interest in the operating data and results they are responsible for. The rest of this discussion is devoted to describing gainsharing in more detail.

### WHAT IS GAINSHARING?

Gainsharing is best thought of as a group incentive and involvement system. It is not just an incentive system, however. Covered employees need some means by which they can express and assert their new-found interest in and responsibility for their work area, or the maximum benefits can not be obtained. The gain is calculated from a predetermined formula that is based in such a way so performance is truly better that it would have been without the gainsharing feature. In this sense, the plan is self-funding. Gains are actual performance increments that the company would not have had without the plan. Finally, the payout of the plan is current (within the same year, at least). This is the part of the definition that excludes most standard profit-sharing plans.

An effective gainsharing system can help solve several types of problems in an organization. Some involvement programs have proceeded successfully for years without anything except casual awards as compensation support. Eventually, though, (and sometimes quite soon) some of the participants will be asking "what's in it for me?" Gainsharing allows you to answer, "Additional pay is in it for you."

## Gainsharing and Teamwork

Gainsharing develops teamwork in places where teamwork has been slow to develop. An obvious improvement can be in teamwork and cooperation between labor and management. Recognizing that there is a reward for everyone if things improve encourages even reluctant members of both groups to cooperate. But the basic tools and structures for cooperation must be present already. Gainsharing also generates teamwork in labor-labor and management-management situations. Where multiple unions are in the same or equivalent plan(s), the incentive to cooperate is clear. Also, a company can overcome intraplant jealousies, whether it is unionized or not, by an appeal to the common good backed by real reward possibilities. The same rivalries can exist in management, for example, operations versus engineering, design versus production, inspection versus production or office versus plant. Gainsharing offers a common language for cooperation.

The creation of a gainsharing plan, if accomplished through a cross-cutting design team, can itself be strong evidence that involvement works where there may have been difficulty generating a good example of success. The possibility of reward may focus groups that otherwise viewed participative management as a mere exercise. The creation of a gainsharing plan is a unique opportunity for a team to go through the entire design-develop-produce-administer cycle.

## Gainsharing and Compensation

A company benefits from introducing the flexible payroll concept, especially if it is subject to cyclical fluctuation in profit performance and thus *ability to pay*. In the base case where wages are totally fixed, a decline in the fortunes of the company leads to a proportionate cut in the work force. But if gainsharing makes up part of the overall compensation, and it partially fluctuates with the business cycle, some cut in payroll is automatic through gainsharing during cyclical downturns. Additional *bonus* money is available to pay during good times. Thus, layoffs can be postponed longer than in the base case. This obviously depends on the formula used. Some argue that the formula should be as insulated from the business cycle as possible. But if the formula used is partially influenced by economic conditions, avoiding layoff is an obtainable benefit.

Perhaps the most important effect of gainsharing is the psychological benefit employees derive from closer identification with the overall fate of the company that occurs with the additional emphasis on performance from gainsharing.

## Gainsharing Plans

There are several types of gainsharing plans in use today (see Figure 10). Gainsharing originated in the United States with the Scanlon Plan in the mid-'30s. It was originally an informal suggestion system whereby some union members gave advice to management on how to keep their company going during the depression. It was later institutionalized and transformed into a bonus plan as it became routinely successful. The Scanlon formula is based on labor cost as a percentage of output value, as variously defined. This incorporates the centrality of the hiring decision; fewer people means fewer to share the pot with. Making do with less people is a common theme. It also includes

**TRADITIONAL GAINSHARING PLANS**

- Scanlon Plan
- Rucker Plan
- Improshare

and now
- Custom *Family of Measures*

**Figure 10.**

price effects, both product price and wage rate. An increase or decrease in product price, everything equal, results in more or less of a bonus. The company gets the exclusive benefit of improvements in the other factors of production, materials, capital, and energy.

In time, other variations on the Scanlon financial approach were developed. The Rucker Plan works off a value added as a percent of product value formula, thus bringing in directly or indirectly the other factors of production. But it still reflects pricing in addition to performance. A version of profit sharing with current (within the year) payout is also used, much the same as Rucker, but easier to explain. It is common to use an *adjusted profit*, which gives attention to the expense items the work force at hand can control and the ones they cannot.

In response to the problem of incorporating nonperformance elements, such as pricing, into the formula, a group of physical formula plans were developed. The most common is Improshare, based on earned hours against standard hours of labor. While eliminating the inclusion of price effects, it goes back to the exclusion of materials, capital, and energy. Some argue that all of them are a function of labor cost, which may be nearly true in some very labor-intensive and underdeveloped businesses.

The most common approach now is a customized plan, using a *family of measures*. These are typically physical measures, or financial measures with inflation adjustment. The typical family might include four to six measures that reflect labor, capital, materials, and/or energy productivity. More advanced plans go beyond productivity and include quality, cycle time, safety, and other parameters in the family.

A gainsharing plan is usually classified by its formula type, but of course various other forms of involvement are also used. Many plans still use the original idea of suggestion systems along with various types of participative teams that directly focus improvement toward the gainsharing measures.

Figure 11 presents information on the prevalence of gainsharing plans in two comprehensive surveys.

## SURVEY RESULTS ON GAINSHARING

**a. Percent That Have in Their Company**

| %(n=1598) | All Sample | Goods Companies | Service Companies |
|---|---|---|---|
| Profit Sharing | 32 | 37 | 28 |
| Individual Incentives | 28 | 27 | 29 |
| Gainsharing | 13 | 20 | 8 |
| Pay for Knowledge | 5 | 8 | 2 |

**b. Overall Performance Ranking**

Percent Rating Good (= 4 or 5 on Five-Point Scale)

| | |
|---|---|
| Pay for Knowledge | 89 |
| Gainsharing | 81 |
| Profit Sharing | 74 |
| Individual Incentives | 73 |

Source: APQC, *People, Performance and Pay* (Houston: American Productivity and Quality Center, 1987).

**Percent That Have in Their Company**

| %(N = 435) | All Sample | Goods Companies | Service Companies |
|---|---|---|---|
| Individual Incentives | 35 | 30 | 39 |
| Profit sharing | 19 | 25 | 14 |
| Gainsharing | 13 | 20 | 8 |
| Pay for Knowledge | 10 | 14 | 7 |

Source: Conference Board, *Variable Pay: New Performance Rewards* (New York: Conference Board, 1990).

**Figure 11.**

## CREATING A CUSTOMIZED PLAN

The bad news about designing your own gainsharing plan is that you need to consider 20 key issues (see Figure 12). The good news is that there are *only 20,* not 47 or 64. With appropri-

---

### CUSTOM GAINSHARING ISSUES

**Planning**
1. Is the organization ready?
2. What are the group or site boundaries?
3. What are the roles of union and government?
4. What is the nature of the design team?

**Design**
5. Employee eligibility
6. Linkage with existing employee involvement
7. Medium of payment
8. Communication: design phase
9. Post-launch communication and administration
10. Frequency of payout
11. Splitting the payout
12. Capping formula elements
13. Share and magnitude

**Formula**
14. Determining performance measures
15. Establishing a baseline
16. Adjusting for capital investment
17. Converting performance to value and aggregation of measures
18. Deficit reserve
19. Including gates in a plan
20. Linking gainsharing to individual compensation

---

**Figure 12.**

ate front-end guidance from top management, a mixed team of amateurs can learn about gainsharing, design its own plan, and launch it in six to nine months, all with a relatively small amount of nonintrusive consultant time.

## Planning Issues

Much of the eventual success of a customized plan comes from the quality of the early planning. Four of the twenty issues can be classified as planning issues:

1. Is the organization ready?

2. What are the group or site boundaries?

3. What are the roles of union and government?

4. What is the nature of the design team?

**1. Is the organization ready?** A definitive answer to this question may not be available, but there are indicators to consider. First, does top management support the concept of pay-for-performance? There will always be someone who says "We already pay folks for maximum performance ... why should be pay even more?" The speaker is usually an executive who personally receives a bonus on top of an already good salary but somehow that is different! As long as the key managers acknowledge that *normal salary* only gets *normal effort* there is room for a gainsharing plan, and the skeptics can be won over.

Readiness also deals with the business cycle. It is foolish to install a gainsharing plan just before a company expects bad financial results. If the company launches the plan, but no one receives a bonus for some time, due to business conditions, everyone will blame gainsharing. Wait until just past the bottom of the business cycle, if you can ascertain that, and then install the plan. The recovery will bring with it good initial payouts for most formula combinations. Readiness also deals with the degree of employee involvement in the organization. Workers, on hearing the announcement of the plan, need to understand how they can contribute to improvements. They must have the training, tools, and permission/empowerment to influence the flow of work and the quality of its accomplishment. The state of involvement does not need to be perfect, but the direction of progress must be clear.

**2. What are the group or site boundaries?** This is one of the most difficult issues. Gainsharing typically is associated with a *site*, a whole, self-contained location. The plan includes everyone: production, shipping, office, management, sanitation workers, etc. A plan that tries to include several sites in the same calculation risks generating the feeling that workers can't control, or even influence the overall result. This is the major fault of organization-wide profit-sharing plans. Workers feel they can't influence the result adequately, and in fact, they are suspicious that those other guys are lazier than they are, thus dragging down the plan potential!

If a company subdivides the plan so that each small work group has its own plan, the real possibility of divisiveness and self-seeking becomes common. Work groups won't take the time to cooperate with upstream and downstream departments or sections of the work process because that takes away from the performance of the group. Clearly, it is necessary to subdivide a site that contains 10,000 workers to prevent the feeling of remoteness. But in a plant with up to 700 workers, a single plan for the site is recommended.

Larger organizations can develop layered plans. In these, workers at a large site are members of two (or in one case, three) groups: the plan for the whole site and a plan for a sub-section. This layering hedges against the self-seeking that comes from multiple plans by having people gain individually from both their own immediate effort and cooperation with other groups or sections.

**3. What are the roles of union and government?** It has already been suggested that management needs to be ready for the concept of pay-for-performance. So does the union also need to be ready? The senior management of the national union may have an opinion on the issue, and certainly a company should discuss it openly with them before proceeding very far. In the United States, however, there is rarely such an opinion; all depends on local issues. Also, the United States has no government or regulatory issue; gainsharing plans are legal and possible everywhere if members of the organization enter into them freely and without baggage left over from other issues. This is not true in many other countries that regulate the permissive range of compensation policy of an organization.

The local union may have suspicions based on a past history of disputes, but it is very rare for a local union to reject out-of-hand the offer of free money. In fact the pride that typically resides in an established local often comes to the surface. The idea of more pay for better performance is treated as a challenge they can't resist. Incredibly, the opportunity is still sometimes lost through incompetent handling by either side of what should be obvious mutual gain.

**4. What is the nature of the design team?** The design team should consist of a cross-section of the site's employees. In a unionized situation, the union(s) should be well represented but not necessarily as much as 50 percent. A team that has to vote is not a team! Management needs representation, typically, professionals such as an accountant, a human resources person, and a process engineer. They bring specific knowledge the team needs in its work. The team must also represent non-organized white-collar staff.

The design team should meet once every week or two for two to four hours, and work on special subgroup projects between meetings. Initially they receive training on the gain-sharing concepts and then break into subgroups to start considering the key issues. Typically the productivity/quality specialist or the human resources person is the committee's secretary in charge of setting up and facilitating the meetings, possibly with the help of an outside consultant.

## Design Issues

Nine other key issues turn up as design issues. Each custom installation has its own additional issues, but these appear everywhere.

5. Employee eligibility

6. Linkage with existing employee involvement

7. Medium of payment

8. Communication: design phase

9. Post-launch communication and administration

10. Frequency of payout

11. Splitting the payout

12. Capping formula elements

13. Share and magnitude

**5. Employee eligibility.** The design team must clearly agree before launch who participates in the plan and who does not. This boundary issue is the main discriminator, but within it there are still some issues. Is it sufficient that an employee worked even briefly in the pay period, or should an employee work half-time or more? Does every employee get a full share, or is it proportional to attendance during the period? Do sick, funeral, or vacation days count? Must the worker be on the payroll at the end of the period to be eligible? The beginning of the period? Are employees on probation or receiving a low performance rating eligible? Are independent contractors working on the site eligible? Part-time employees? Student aides?

**6. Linkage with existing employee involvement efforts.** We say that gainsharing is an involvement system, and readiness means receptivity to, if not experience in, involvement. The aims of the approaches to involvement have to mesh with the gainsharing formula's featured parameters. The employees must understand these parameters and see how they can do something towards improving them. This may require not only sensitivity in the design of the gainsharing system, but even some changes in the preexisting employee involvement systems. Such a simple matter as how the gainsharing design team fits or ranks as compared to the employee involvement steering committee can cause trouble, unless of course, they are the same.

**7. Medium of payment.** Traditionally, gainsharing plans pay in cash. Cash is the most generally useful commodity, and its value is easy to identify. But other types of rewards are found. The advantage of merchandise is that a large company can buy it at a discount; Cash presumably cannot be. It also has *monument value*, that is, at home, it invites comments and praise to the worker and implicitly to the supplying company. Some companies are now using travel credit plans with the same advantages as merchandise and perhaps at even deeper discounts.

**8. Communication during design phase.** In a sense, the design team represents the rest of the organization, so they must effectively communicate back to their constituents. They may even seek volunteers not on the team to help with difficult issues. They have to use good judgement because many of the recommendations of the design committee still have to be finally accepted by the company's top management and sometimes the union membership.

If the design team has issued effective progress reports, then everyone will easily understand the program when it launches. The launch needs to be multimedia. Some people only read, some people listen only to peers, some listen only to managers and some younger ones only believe videos. Do them all!

**9. Post-launch communication and administration.** Very often the design team stays on as program administrator after the plan is launched. Each time period, the team arranges for the calculation of a new set of performance results and consequent payout. They also explain what happened and what that implies for the improvement activities and teams for the next period. The team also recommends on disputes concerning eligibility and formula calculation. Once a year, they should review the measures, set new baselines if that is provided for, see if the plan is still consistent with the company's strategic direction, and make sure that employees still understand and accept it.

**10. Frequency of payout.** Gainsharing plans pay out annually or more frequently; otherwise, they don't meet the definition of gainsharing. Most new plans in the United States pay out monthly or quarterly. A few pay weekly and a few pay annually. The results can, of course, be calculated more frequently than the payout. Everything equal, more frequent payout means smaller checks, less frequent payout means larger checks. The committee chooses between more frequent and larger reinforcement. A smaller check means the bonus might find its way into routine household expenditures and have no monument value. A large check can buy something with monument value, but there are times during the year when it's easy to forget there is a plan around.

**11. Splitting the payout.** In the United States the normal split is that everyone gets the same percent of pay. Thus, a high-ranking person gets several times the bonus a lower-ranking person does, regardless of who made the suggestions or spearheaded the improvement effort. This is the result of an outrageous quirk in U.S. law that forces recalculation of the overtime basis if any other gainsharing basis is used.

Outside the United States, the overwhelming choice is to pay the same absolute amount of money to everyone. The base wage takes care of differences in education, experience, and basic skill required. Gainsharing should reward those who have done the most for incremental improvement, and that could be anyone at any level.

**12. Capping formula elements.** Should the formula element(s) have caps on either the up or down-side? If the formula element represents a true gain, as it should, the company should want unlimited improvement. But some measures are immature or imprecise. Beyond a certain level the company is sometimes nervous about factors outside of their control that enter the picture. For example, if energy use is a formula factor, many of the reasons for unusually high or low use are out of employee control. So energy use might be capped on both sides — it can gain you no more than $x$ and lose you no more than $y$.

**13. Share and magnitude.** Calculating *frontwards* it is easy to say that 50-50 sharing between the company and the workers sounds fair. But with some formulas, 50 percent may be too much or too little. Thus after setting the formula parameters and bases, *backward* calculations are usually made. How much can the company reasonably expect in total improvement? For that level of total improvement, workers could reasonably be paid $x$ percent. That back-calculates into, for example, a 60–40 sharing basis.

In the *People, Performance, and Pay* study,[3] the median payout from a gainsharing plan was about 8 percent of pay with a normal range of 5 to 12 percent. Less than 5 percent (for a good year) runs the risk of being considered cheap. Over 12 percent runs the risk of "leaving money on the table," that is, paying more than was necessary to get the level of effort. These numbers clearly change from culture to culture and also depend heavily on the adequacy of the base wage level.

## Formula Issues in Custom Gainsharing Plans

Finally, there are seven direct issues that help determine the best formula to use:

14. Determining performance measures

15. Establishing a baseline

16. Adjusting for capital investment

17. Converting performance to value and aggregation of measures

18. Deficit reserve

19. Including gates in a plan

20. Linking gainsharing to individual compensation

**14. Determining performance measures.** Traditional gainsharing practice measures improvement with one formula. Profit sharing, not surprisingly, uses profit. The Scanlon plan originally used labor cost as a percentage of sales. Improshare also measures only labor productivity. Business, however, is not that simple. A better guide to measure selection is the objectives of the strategic plan. There, it is typical to have five to six key objectives that reflect the critical concerns of the organization. If that is what is most important, the measures of these objectives should be the most important measures you can use. Reward systems should encourage or motivate employees to do the most important things well. Thus the measures for gainsharing should be measures of the five to six key objectives — a *family* of measures rather than one or two. Figure 13 lists commonly used measures. Figure 14 shows some company-specific measures.

The word *family* is appropriate in another sense. Just as the members of a human family can act both as independent humans and together as a unit, so can a company interpret and act on the measures individually or as a balanced unit. And some measures are more important than others, that is, they are weighted more heavily or have more reward power than others.

Another important feature of a measurement system is that the people it measures must be able to understand it and control it, or at least be able to influence it. Thus, the top of the organization needs one family of measures, the operating divisions need another, still other key departments or sections need another. Rotating the matrix, key processes that cut across the departments of an organization also need their own family of measures. Everyone in the organization works with a family of measures of appropriate scale that is based on the strategic objectives that apply to that work group.

---

### POSSIBLE MEASURES FOR GAINSHARING

- labor productivity
- energy productivity
- materials productivity, yield, scrap rate
- capital productivity, inventory turnover
- first pass yield, rework
- returns, adjustments
- misdeliveries, late deliveries
- cycle time
- unplanned downtime
- cost of service
- resource utilization
- team participation
- customer satisfaction survey
- safety
- housekeeping, cleanliness
- innovation, creativity
- new products, ideas, suggestions
- documentation timeliness, accuracy
- market share
- effluent measures
- process interruptions, delays

---

**Figure 13.**

**15. Establishing a baseline.** You cannot demonstrate improvement with one observation. You need to establish a reference point or base in addition to the actual observation. Traditional gainsharing measures the parameter at the beginning of the plan and freezes the base at that level forever. Thus, as performance slowly improves the rewards get bigger, even though the effort to develop the improvement may even

### EXAMPLES OF COMPANY GAINSHARING MEASURES

**A large chemical company uses:**
- continuous product yield
- continuous product error reduction
- batch product cycle time
- batch product recycle percent
- energy use
- maintenance salvage
- tools and supplies use
- waste water cost

**A large metal processor uses:**
- direct labor productivity
- scrap rate
- special ingredients use
- packaging use
- truck fleet turnaround time
- worker's compensation costs

**A large paper mill uses:**
- employee-hours per ton
- steam use
- shipping on-time
- sewer loss
- lost-time accidents
- maintenance cost

**A food warehouse uses:**
- throughput per hour
- warehouse damage
- lift truck costs
- energy cost
- incomplete shipments
- inventory discrepancy
- safety

**A software development group uses:**
- project cost vs. budget
- quality rating
- on-time incentive
- life-cycle cost (delayed)

Source: Carl G. Thor, "Knowledge Worker Gainsharing," in *Handbook for Productivity Measurement and Improvement*, William F. Christopher and Carl G. Thor, eds. (Portland, Ore.: Productivity Press, 1993), p. 8.4.

**Figure 14.**

be less than before. Today's employees are being rewarded for the ideas of their grandfathers.

Most companies would not accept such a situation. At the other extreme, however, the work force may not be happy with instant adjustment of the base every time there was a major improvement, as there would then be no reward. Normal practice is to partially adjust the base at predetermined periodic intervals. Thus next year's base might be half way between last year's actual and this year's actual. Or, a rolling average of the last two years is recalculated each quarter when new data arrives. This is done by taking away data from that quarter two years ago and adding the new quarter.

Most gainsharing formula elements are continuous functions. That is, if the base of labor productivity is 23 widgets per hour, reaching 25 pays something, 26 pays something more, and so on. But some plans are binary or goal-based. Here 23 might be the base; reward occurs if 25.0 is reached, but 24.9 or less gets you nothing and 25.1 or more gets you only what the reward was for 25.

**16. Adjusting for capital investment.** Some elements of the formula are *automatically* helped by capital investment. The relevant employees did nothing to improve the system and were not expected to do anything. Here the company justified capital investment based on these labor savings. It would be counter-productive to have to pay gainsharing on this sort of gain. Thus the base is adjusted upward based on the expected *automatic* effect of the new equipment or tool. Sometimes the adjustment only reaches 80 percent of the total effect. Twenty percent is left on the table to encourage the workers to accept and integrate the new machinery quickly.

**17. Converting performance to value and aggregation of measures.** The easier conversion of a measured result to dollar value is the binary goal list. The company gives predetermined dollar values for each attainment, adds up the successes for each time period and disperses the money. Examples of the aggregations are shown in Figure 15.

**CONVERSION OF PERFORMANCE TO VALUE**

**a. Binary Function Aggregation: Group of Field Service Reps**

| Measure | New Data | Target | Make? | $ Per Person if Make | $ Made |
|---|---|---|---|---|---|
| Weighted calls per rep | 15.17 | 15.00 | Yes | 600 | 600 |
| Service cost per weighted call | 85.27 | 83.00 | No | 300 | 0 |
| Time between visits | 4.01 | 4.00 | Yes | 300 | 300 |
| Customer satisfaction | 88.1 | 87.5 | Yes | 200 | 200 |
| Lag between job completion and paperwork | 4.19 | 3.80 | No | 100 | 0 |
| Total Benefit | | | | 1,500 | 1,100 |

**Figure 15.**

In the simple measures list where the measures are continuous functions, the measures around cost are usually easy. The value to the organization of saving a dollar is usually approximately $1.00. The issue is a little more complex if the measure is physical. For example, saving a ton of scrap requires someone to look up the value of the material being scrapped. Other measures might require a more complex but still explicit calculation, such as scheduling benefits. And finally, for some unknowables the value translation has to be a guess or a token value. How do you translate the value of gaining one point on a customer satisfaction survey, having an R&D scientist publish one more paper, or gaining a higher safety or housekeeping rating?

**b. Continuous Function Aggregation: Group of Field
Service Reps**

| Measure | Base Data | New Data | Improve-ment | $/Unit of Improvement | Actual Benefit |
|---|---|---|---|---|---|
| Weighted calls per rep | 14.32 | 15.17 | .85 | $50K/1 | $42.5K |
| Service cost per weighted call | 83.21 | 85.27 | (2.06) | $15K/1 | ($30.9K) |
| Time between visits | 3.70 | 4.01 | .31 | $30K/1 | $9.3K |
| Customer satisfaction | 86.3 | 88.1 | 1.8 | $5K/1 | $9.0K |
| Lag between job completion and paperwork | 3.98 | 4.19 | (.21) | $40K/1 | (8.4K) |
| Total Benefit | | | | | $21.5K |

**Figure 15. (Cont.)**

**18. Deficit reserve.** If each time period is free-standing, the deficit reserve is not an issue. But if partial payments are to be made, the risk from the company's point-of-view is that they will make premature payouts they cannot recapture from the employees. Thus, the company withholds some percentage (25 percent normally) until the end of the total period, then distributes this reserve in the final calculation. In the typical case, quarterly payouts are made, but the settlement period is only the fiscal year. An illustration of the procedure appears in Figure 16.

**19. Including gates in a plan.** Sometimes an overriding constraint wipes out any chance of a gainsharing payout.

| | 1Q | 2Q | 3Q | 4Q | Year-End Payout Summary |
|---|---|---|---|---|---|
| **ILLUSTRATION OF DEFICIT RESERVE** | | | | | |
| Example of Reserve Calculation and Payment Schedule | | | | | |
| 50% of gain | 5,000 | 2,000 | (1,000) | 5,000 | --- |
| 25% Reserve | 1,250 | 500 | --- | 1,250 | --- |
| Direct Payout | 3,750 | 1,500 | 0 | 3,750 | 9,000 |
| Cumulative Reserve | 1,250 | 1,750 | 750 | 2,000 | 2,000 |
| Eligible Payroll | 90K | 90K | 90K | 90K | --- |
| Bonus | 4.2% | 1.7% | 0% | 4.2% | 3.1% of annual payroll |

**Figure 16.**

For example, a plan might pay according to a predetermined schedule, but if the company loses money in that period, no gainsharing is allowed, no matter how much improvement has occurred. This is called a *profit gate*. Sometimes there is a *quality gate*. The family of measures is based on productivity and operational variables, but if the quality or customer satisfaction score goes down, no payment is made. *Safety* is also used as a gate. It is generally preferable to include those variables directly in the formula. It is viewed as unfair to penalize workers who have made massive improvements at that plant just because the corporate profit manipulations have turned up negative.

**20. Link to individual compensation policy.** Most organizations have an individual *merit pay* that in the United

States at least, is more likely to be unofficial inflation adjustment rather than true merit pay.

Some organizations are starting to give the true merit pay as a one-shot bonus rather than as permanent pay increase. This reflects the project or episodic nature of many of the activities that a quality effort engenders and avoids further increasing what is often already too high a base pay to be internationally competitive.

The individual plan that fits best with gainsharing is pay-for-knowledge (PFK). This allows an increment of pay level based on what employees are certified to do, not what they may be doing right now. Thus, an electrician who can also weld makes more than a single-skill electrician who at this moment is doing identical work. A member of an autonomous work team who can do every job on that team makes more than a member who can only do three of the eight jobs, regardless of current work slot. It is worth paying for this extra skill because it buys a lot of extra flexibility for the company, not only for vacation coverage but also to fill slots of retirees and allow expansion without a pause to train completely new crews or teams.

If PFK is paired with gainsharing, everyone has incentive to cooperate towards the big strategic issues. A more relaxed team member can simply get base pay and gainsharing. The more ambitious individual will also cooperate with and get gainsharing, but can always go to night school or take special training to climb the certification ladder.

## LIMITATIONS OF GAINSHARING

Of course, gainsharing is not a panacea. Many compensation problems cannot be solved with gainsharing. For example, the gap between executive compensation and worker compensation might be too wide. Gainsharing can only lower the gap if the executives are left out of the plan, which is not usually a good idea. If the workers' base salaries are too high, then adding the possibility of still more pay may not seem to help much. If gainsharing significantly stimulates performance, an overall better solution might result. But basic competitiveness is first a function of basic wage rate level.

Gainsharing alone does not help individual workers who are most challenged by the idea of being best in their work group or work force. But gainsharing plans often fit well with skill pay or pay-for-knowledge plans where individuals are encouraged to apply for additional certifications or master additional skills.

Finally, product and business cycles can kill an otherwise-good plan. Though it is advisable to use measures that are as sheltered as possible from cyclical factors, that is sometimes quite difficult. When the volume through the plant goes down many "bad" things can happen. In theory, a slower pace of production may help other members of the family of measures such as first-run quality level or cycle time from order-placement. But if the formula is singularly dedicated to a bottom-line type of number, then when this number goes south, so does the gainsharing payout. Starting a plan and its formula base(s) just past the bottom of a business cycle is not always possible, but it can help get the plan off to a good start.

# 5

# SUMMARY AND CONCLUSION

1. A high-performance organization must be responsive to customers, using its planning processes to focus improvement action on meeting customer needs through effective employee teams.

2. Research shows that employee involvement efforts enhance productivity, quality, and customer satisfaction.

3. Employee involvement mainly contains information-sharing, knowledge and skill development, rewards and recognition, and power-sharing.

4. The two major kinds of employee teams are special purpose teams and permanent operating teams. Each has several variations and styles.

5. Team effectiveness is measured in three general ways: customer perception, internal or upstream excellence, and the team's own characteristics and operation.

6. Performance measurement and reward take place at the top (executive) and the bottom (individual) of the organization, but the part that is now receiving all the attention (teams, departments, business processes, locations) is not well-measured and there are few effective group rewards.

7. Customized gainsharing plans, based on a family of measures, can provide a solution to this omission that ties together the whole organization.

8. Gainsharing systems can be developed by an organization with ample attention to 20 points grouped into planning, design, and formula issues.

# BIBLIOGRAPHY

## Studies:

1. Center for Effective Organizations, University of Southern California and American Productivity & Quality Center. *Employee Involvement in America.* Houston: American Productivity & Quality Center, 1989.

2. Conference Board. *Variable Pay: New Performance Rewards.* New York: Conference Board, 1990.

3. American Productivity & Quality Center. *People, Performance and Pay.* Houston: American Productivity and Quality Center, 1987.

4. Federal Quality Institute. "Employee Involvement and Quality Management," U.S. Government Printing Office, 1993.

## Other:

5. Belcher, John G. *Gain Sharing.* Houston: Gulf Publishing, 1991.

6. Boyett, J.H. and H.P. Conn. *Maximum Performance Management.* Macomb, Ill.: Glenbridge Publishing, 1988.

7. Thor, Carl G. "Integrating Service Productivity & Quality Through Measurement," *Continuous Journey,* October/November 1992.

8. The model used in Figure 1 was developed in collaboration with Fidelma Donahue of the Office of Personnel Management and Fran Nurthen and JoAnn Barsis of the Army Corps of Engineers.

## ABOUT THE AUTHOR

Carl G. Thor is president of Jarrett Thor International. Previously he served as president and vice chairman of the American Productivity & Quality Center, where he was responsible for the Center's work in productivity measurement and gainsharing. Earlier, he held international and corporate headquarters positions with Anderson Clayton and Company and with Humble Oil and Refining Company. He has led several industry studies and statistical research projects and has worked with a wide variety of organizations to create and improve productivity and quality management, measurement, and reward systems.

Mr. Thor has published many articles and papers, and is co-editor and a contributing author of *Handbook for Productivity Measurement and Improvement.* He is a director of the Fundacion Mexicana para la Calidad Total, and is a fellow of the World Confederation of Productivity Science. He holds a B.A. from Oberlin College and an M.B.A. in statistics from the University of Chicago.

# The Management Master Series

The *Management Master Series* offers business managers leading-edge information on the best contemporary management practices. Written by highly respected authorities, each short "briefcase book" addresses a specific topic in a concise, to-the-point presentation, using both text and illustrations. These are ideal books for busy managers who want to get the whole message quickly.

## Set 1 — Great Management Ideas

1. *Management Alert: Don't Reform—Transform!*
   Michael J. Kami

   Transform your corporation: adapt faster, be more productive, perform better.

2. *Vision, Mission, Total Quality: Leadership Tools for Turbulent Times*
   William F. Christopher
   Build your vision and mission to achieve world class goals.

3. *The Power of Strategic Partnering*
   Eberhard E. Scheuing
   Take advantage of the strengths in your customer-supplier chain.

4. *New Performance Measures*
   Brian H. Maskell
   Measure service, quality, and flexibility with methods that address your customers' needs.

5. *Motivating Superior Performance*
   Saul W. Gellerman
   Use these key factors—nonmonetary as well as monetary—to improve employee performance.

6. *Doing and Rewarding: Inside a High-Performance Organization*
   Carl G. Thor
   Design systems to reward superior performance and encourage productivity.

## Set 2 — Total Quality

7. ***The 16-Point Strategy for Productivity and Total Quality***
William F. Christopher and Carl G. Thor

   Essential points you need to know to improve the performance of your organization.

8. ***The TQM Paradigm: Key Ideas That Make It Work***
Derm Barrett

   Get a firm grasp of the world-changing ideas behind the Total Quality movement.

9. ***Process Management: A Systems Approach to Total Quality***
Eugene H. Melan

   Learn how a business process orientation will clarify and streamline your organization's capabilities.

10. ***Practical Benchmarking for Mutual Improvement***
Carl G. Thor

    Discover a down-to-earth approach to benchmarking and building useful partnerships for quality.

11. ***Mistake-Proofing: Designing Errors Out***
Richard B. Chase and Douglas M. Stewart

    Learn how to eliminate errors and defects at the source with inexpensive poka-yoke devices and staff creativity.

12. ***Communicating, Training, and Developing for Quality Performance***
Saul W. Gellerman

    Gain quick expertise in communication and employee development basics.

These books are sold in sets. Each set is $85.00 plus $5.00 shipping and handling. Future sets will cover such topics as Customer Service, Leadership, and Innovation. For complete details, call 800-394-6868 or fax 800-394-6286.

## BOOKS FROM PRODUCTIVITY PRESS

Productivity Press provides individuals and companies with materials they need to achieve excellence in quality, productivity and the creative involvement of all employees. Through sets of learning tools and techniques, Productivity supports continuous improvement as a vision, and as a strategy. Many of our leading-edge products are direct source materials translated into English for the first time from industrial leaders around the world. Call toll-free 1-800-394-6868 for our free catalog.

### Handbook for Productivity Measurement and Improvement
*William F. Christopher and Carl G. Thor, eds.*
An unparalleled resource! In over 100 chapters, nearly 80 front-runners in the quality movement reveal the evolving theory and specific practices of world-class organizations. Spanning a wide variety of industries and business sectors, they discuss quality and productivity in manufacturing, service industries, profit centers, administration, nonprofit and government institutions, health care and education. Contributors include Robert C. Camp, Peter F. Drucker, Jay W. Forrester, Joseph M. Juran, Robert S. Kaplan, John W. Kendrick, Yasuhiro Monden, and Lester C. Thurow. Comprehensive in scope and organized for easy reference, this compendium belongs in every company and academic institution concerned with business and industrial viability.
ISBN 1-56327-007-2 / 1344 pages / $90.00 / Order HPM-B238

### The Idea Book
### Improvement Through TEI (Total Employee Involvement)
*Japan Human Relations Association*
At last, a book showing how to create Total Employee Involvement (TEI) and get hundreds of ideas from each employee every year to improve every aspect of your organization. Gathering improvement ideas from your entire workforce is a must for global competitiveness. *The Idea Book*, heavily illustrated, is a hands-on teaching tool for workers and supervisors to refer to again and again. Perfect for study groups, too.
ISBN 0-915299-22-4 / 232 pages / $55.00 / Order IDEA-B238

**The Unshackled Organization**
Facing the Challenge of Unpredictability Through
Spontaneous Reorganization
*Jeffrey Goldstein*
Managers should not necessarily try to solve all the internal problems within their organizations; intervention may help in the short term, but in the long run may inhibit true problem-solving change from taking place. And change is the real goal. Through change comes real hope for improvement. Goldstein explores how change happens within an organization using some of the most leading-edge scientific and social theories about change and reveals that only through "self organization" can natural, lasting change occur. This book is a pragmatic guide for managers, executives, consultants, and other change agents.
ISBN 1-56327-048-X / 208 pages / $25.00 / Order UO-B238

**Kaizen Teian 1**
Developing Systems for Continuous Improvement Through
Employee Suggestions
*Japan Human Relations Association (ed.)*
Especially relevant for middle and upper managers, this book focuses on the role of managers as catalysts in spurring employee ideas and facilitating their implementation. It explains how to run a proposal program on a day-to-day basis and outlines the policies that support a "bottom-up" system of innovation and defines the three main objectives of kaizen teian: to build participation, develop individual skills, and achieve higher profits.
ISBN 0-915299-89-5 / 217 pages / $40.00 / Order KT1-B238

TO ORDER: Write, phone, or fax Productivity Press, Dept. BK, P.O. Box 13390, Portland, OR 97213-0390, phone 1-800-394-6868, fax 1-800-394- 6286. Send check or charge to your credit card (American Express, Visa, MasterCard accepted).

U.S. ORDERS: Add $5 shipping for first book, $2 each additional for UPS surface delivery. Add $5 for each AV program containing 1 or 2 tapes; add $12 for each AV program containing 3 or more tapes. We offer attractive quantity discounts for bulk purchases of individual titles; call for more information.

INTERNATIONAL ORDERS: Write, phone, or fax for quote and indicate shipping method desired. For international callers, telephone number is 503-235-0600 and fax number is 503-235-0909. Prepayment in U.S. dollars must accompany your order (checks must be drawn on U.S. banks). When quote is returned with payment, your order will be shipped promptly by the method requested.

NOTE: Prices are in U.S. dollars and are subject to change without notice.